THE

FAMILY BUSINESS

WHISPERER

BY

DAVID SPECHT

WITH TANEIL SPECHT

visit us at: *AdvisingGenerations.com*

--

Edited by: Joe Bailie and Julie Geilman Mitchell

Cover design and typesetting by: Joshua Kessie

--

Library of Congress Cataloging-in Publication Data:

Specht, David, author.
The Family Business Whisperer / David Specht

Pages 167 cm

Includes index

ISBN: 978-0-9965979-2-0 (paperback)

First Edition

Printed in the United States of America

TO MY WIFE TANEIL AND MY CHILDREN
MAKALEY, DAMON, REICHERT, JHETT AND
LIBERTY. YOUR SUPPORT AND UNCONDITIONAL
LOVE INSPIRES ME.

TO MY PARENTS, CLIFF AND CHRIS SPECHT
AND MY SIBLINGS, AMIE, D.J. AND JACLYN.
YOU ALWAYS TOLD ME I COULD ACCOMPLISH
ANYTHING AND I BELIEVED YOU.

AND TO JIM ABEL FOR MAKING IT POSSIBLE
TO TEACH THE NEXT GENERATION OF FAMILY
BUSINESS LEADERS AT THE UNIVERSITY OF
NEBRASKA.

AND FINALLY, TO ALL OF THE FAMILIES THAT
I HAVE CONSULTED WITH. I HONOR THE TRUST
YOU HAVE PUT IN ME AND THIS BOOK IS
DEDICATED TO YOU.

CONTENTS

SPECHT

PREFACE

The path that I have chosen in life has never been the easy way. Whether it was choosing to walk on to the basketball team in college, spending two years in South America as a missionary or getting married and starting a family before graduating college. I've always pursued opportunities that people questioned as unattainable or just plain hard.

I became interested in working with multi-generational family businesses when I was finishing my graduate degree in Tax and Financial Planning at San Diego State University. I needed one elective class to finish my degree. I decided to take a course in Family Business Management from Carmen Bianchi and my perspective on what I wanted to do with my professional life changed forever.

This course blended the financial and the non-financial issues that business owning families face and gave me the idea that I could make a job out of helping families to stay families, while perpetuating their business legacies.

Family businesses are a special part of the global economy. These businesses are all about people working, sacrificing, struggling and also being successful TOGETHER. I observe families that love building great operations, teaching their kids the value of work and responsibility. I also see families torn apart due to a lack of communication and no coordinated plan for ownership or management.

I often think to myself, how can I help prevent families from this pain? This question drives me to consult, write and speak all over the world. It drives me to create the Inspired Questions—For Family

Business Mobile App, the GenerationalBusiness360 process and now to write, The Family Business Whisperer.

This feels like a calling for me because every family is a unique puzzle. With each family that I touch, I realize that I have an opportunity to influence them individually, as a family, their employees and the community where their business is located.

This work is a labor of love. I hope that something in this book gives you the desire to make choices and plans to Preserve Your Family and Perpetuate Your Business.

INTRODUCTION

The Family Business Whisperer is a nickname that was given to me by a writer in Omaha, NE who was interviewing me for a story. To me The Family Business Whisperer isn't about me, it's about a process that each of us can go through to ask the right questions, pursue the appropriate conversations and implement the best solutions for us personally and for our businesses.

The Family Business Whisperer is a compilation of articles and stories that are meant to assist business-owning families and the professionals that advise them. The book is organized in a way that encourages you to think introspectively about the "Inspired Question" at the end of each chapter and then to allow you to reflect and create an action plan based on what you have read. You can then commit to how you will implement solutions based on what you have learned.

The purpose for this book is to lead you to an intentional planning process that ultimately preserves your family relationships and perpetuates your business legacy.

1

THE POWER OF AN INSPIRED QUESTION
FOR FAMILY BUSINESS

Inspired Questions lead to Inspired Answers.

—DAVID A. BEDNAR

very night I would come home from the University to our basement apartment and find my exhausted wife and newborn little girl. Each evening I would hold my baby in my arms and look into her eyes and anxiety would fill my body. What was my problem? What was I afraid of? This went on for a week or so and then I decided to confide in a university professor that I had great respect for. I told him, "Every time I look into her eyes I worry that I will not have all of the answers that she will need to life's questions. I'm twenty-three, this is my first child and I can't afford to mess this up." Sensing my anxiety he gave me this counsel, "David, it isn't as important that you have all the answers as it is to make sure you have all the right questions."

This was not necessarily the advice I was hoping for, especially since I didn't understand what he really meant. I wanted some concrete answer, "If you read this or do this, it will work out." He didn't give that to me.

Over the ensuing weeks and months I thought about his counsel and began developing questions, then worked at using those questions to pursue knowledge and inspiration on behalf of my little girl and myself. One example was, "In what ways will my actions demonstrate the love and respect I have for her mother?" It was through this exercise that I began to realize the power in an "Inspired Question."

This advice set me on a path personally that calmed my worries and empowered me to act rather than be paralyzed with fear. Over the years I began integrating this process of developing "Inspired Questions" and utilizing them as I worked as a strategy consultant to business-owning families.

So what are the characteristics of an Inspired Question?

- It encourages honest sharing
- It is open ended (Not Yes/No)
- It doesn't have a "right answer"
- It requires reflection and often the
  answer may evolve over time

Throughout this book you will be presented with an Inspired Question at the end of each chapter. Ponder on how you might respond to the questions and then write your reflection and make a commitment to do something with what you've learned. The pattern of learning, reflecting and then committing to take action will be key to this information leading you closer to family business continuity.

The hope is that the power of Inspired Questions will lead you through a journey of introspection and examination helping you to formulate a plan which perpetuates first your family and subsequently your business.

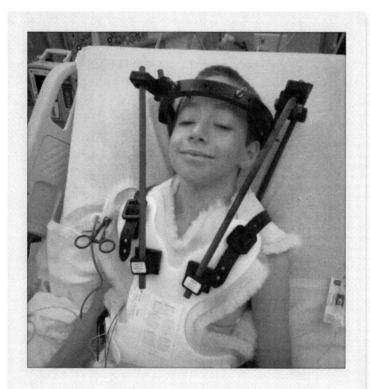

Prayers, Collaboration + Miracles - 2015

2

A CASE FOR COLLABORATION

Coming together is a beginning, staying together
is progress, and working together is success.

—HENRY FORD

As you consider the path towards perpetuating your family business, you will need to decide on the level of collaboration you should expect of your professional advisers. To illustrate the importance of collaboration, I'd like to share a personal story.

In 2003 my wife gave birth to a handsome baby boy. After just a few weeks my wife and I noticed that our newborn son consistently held his head tilted to one side. We took him to the doctor and the diagnosis was our son, Damon, had a muscle spasm called torticollis. If we stretched the muscles of his neck through different therapy exercises it would help and eventually he would grow out of it.

Though my wife was consistent with the stretching and we had him examined by a family friend who was a chiropractor nothing really seemed to improve his condition. At about eighteen months of age his pediatrician recommended x-rays. The anomalies that these scans revealed lead us to Children's Hospital in San Diego for a CT scan. It was discovered that Damon actually had a spinal deformity called hemi-vertebrae. A rare congenital bone disorder that was made more complicated by the fact that while most people have one or two hemi-vertebrae Damon had as many as eight, depending on how you classified several unusual bone formations in his upper back and neck. The final doctor analysis was that there was nothing we could do to help him. It was much too complex to operate on without being able to guarantee that it would improve Damon's quality of life.

We left the hospital feeling helpless, angry and afraid for our son's future. All we could do was pray, watch him grow and hope that the curvature in his spine didn't get worse.

Needless to say the verdict of "there's nothing you can do for him" didn't sit too well with us as parents. Our bodies are amazing in their capacities to adapt and heal, especially those of children. We were lead to other professionals who helped us with therapies that would help Damon's muscles counteract the twist his bones wanted to put on his body. But the reality was that there were no permanent solutions to the challenge that Damon was facing.

We continued to visit expert surgeons as we routinely x-rayed Damon's spine while he grew. The resulting analysis was always the same, surgery would be the last thing to be attempted in Damon's situation. He was healthy and happy and other than a few 'cosmetic' things created by his head tilt he suffered very few repercussions from his highly unusual skeletal structure. An occasional migraine, but otherwise we considered ourselves very lucky.

Fast-forward a few years and Damon is now eleven years old, we have moved and are living in a different area of the country and visiting a new group of specialists for Damon. He has only had x-rays for several years and in the course of routine scans to evaluate his spine his new doctor decides to order a CT scan, his last one was when he was about two years old. During the evaluation appointment the doctor enters with a very serious look on his face and provides a grim diagnosis. A piece of bone from Damon's abnormally shaped vertebrae is now putting pressure on his brain stem and spinal cord such that there is no spinal fluid flowing in that area of his neck. He has virtually no insulation in the area that controls breathing and heart function. Any serious collision or hard fall would probably paralyze him, and sudden death in patients in his situation is not uncommon. Emergency surgery is the safest course of action.

The diagnosis and recommendation came from a wonderful pediatric spine surgeon at Shriner's Hospital in Portland, Oregon. He asked for permission to collaborate with a neurosurgeon that he really respected, but this surgeon worked at Doernbecher Children's Hospital. We agreed and ultimately ended up doing the surgery at Oregon Health Science University. Yes, you are counting right; three hospitals are now involved.

Worried, but hopeful we brought Damon in for surgery. On the day of the operation we had two surgeons, three hospitals, and eight other professionals involved in a surgery that would drag on for nine grueling hours. All of this collaboration, effort and care for one boy, my boy. We were humbled, but still very concerned. This level of collaboration was extraordinary, it was done for my son and I will forever be grateful. Damon emerged from the surgery with a halo that he would wear for four months, but the bone that was causing the problem was removed and vertebrae C1 to C4 were fused to provide stability and straighten his head tilt. Spinal fluid returned to its proper flow, all expectations point to a safe and normal life.

So what does this story have to do with your succession plan? What can be learned and applied from this?

Generational business transitions of ownership and management are processes that are sensitive both for family relationships and also to the business. We do all that we can to manage our problems and work through solutions heeding the good counsel from advisers. Ultimately though, these transitions may require the courage of your current professional team to incorporate specialists more intricately in the process. The communication among the team is crucial to set expectations and for every member of the team to know their role. (If the surgeons had given us an expectation of two hours for the surgery, it would have been torture for us as we moved into hours five, six and beyond.) After the experts had completed Damon's surgery, his full care was returned to us. We brought him home and worked with him over many weeks of healing and rehabilitation. When all is said and done it isn't their family or business, it's yours and you are the one who has to live with it.

Here are three parallels between the collaboration we experienced with the surgery and the collaboration that needs to take place during the succession planning process:

| There is a place for specialists and a place for generalists

Just as we didn't fire our primary care doctor to work exclusively with specialists, so you should consider adding professionals to your advising team as you look more closely at ownership and management succession, while maintaining those relationships with advisors who have earned your trust. Though your banker and accountant may be excellent in their respective fields, management and leadership may not be their domain. Having each professional know their role and be held accountable to one another will be just as paramount for you in your transition-planning journey as it was crucial for my son in his surgery.

The original identification of challenges or problem areas often begin with the 'generalists', but it is only when those difficulties are turned over to the practiced hands of specialists that some solutions can be found.

2 The planning process is only as good as it's weakest team member

Demanding collaboration among your professional advisers may seem more expensive at first, but the work product you receive will be far superior. If the anesthesiologist who was responsible for keeping Damon sedated while the neurosurgeon performed the delicate operation on his vertebrae and spine wasn't able to keep him from flinching in pain the results could have been disastrous. When you have competent professionals reviewing each other's work and crafting a plan that achieves your personal and professional goals while minimizing taxes and bringing order to what can be a chaotic time for a family, let alone a business, it is worth it.

3 Unique situations sometimes require specialized tools

You need more than a stethoscope and thermometer to perform neurosurgery. Just as we didn't expect to find the equipment to help Damon in our general practitioners office, so your family should not rely on professionals that are not properly equipped with the experience, expertise and aptitude to provide your family with a process that will generate a result that you are proud of. In searching out consultants some things you may want to consider looking for are those that have experience with similar levels of complexity. Example: If your family has 50+ shareholders and significant complexity in the governance structures, you will want to make sure you are working with someone that has many repetitions with similar issues.

Similarly if you are pursuing complex gifting strategies that lean heavily on irrevocable trusts to minimize tax and maximize the wealth that can be transferred, you will want to work with an attorney that has created many of these types of trusts and knows the ins and outs of what makes them work and what can make them problematic.

My recommendation is that you make a commitment to collaboration. Is it more expensive? It may seem that way at the outset, but you will end up with a better outcome and product as professionals collaborate and hold each other accountable to do the very best for the family and the business. I guess it goes back to the old adage; sometimes you get what you pay for. In looking for neurosurgeons would you go bargain shopping? We didn't either.

REFLECTIONS

COMMITMENTS

Treasures in Grandpa Wells' Shop

3

YOUR NEW LENS

*What you see and what you hear depends a
great deal on where you are standing. It also
depends on what sort of person you are.*

—C.S. LEWIS

Years ago, as a young family business consultant, I struggled to get families to execute the technical elements of their management plan. As I look back, the key mistake was assuming that the controlling owner had all of the power and influence in executing a continuity plan. What I learned was that all participants in the family operation needed to be understood and given some kind of a voice in the process, only then would the carefully crafted plan move forward with power and impact.

One key tool that helped me to assess the fears, desires and goals of all of these constituents is a model that focuses on the human dynamics of the family business system. Renato Tagiuri and John Davis use a Venn diagram (3 overlapping circles) to help explain the complexities between Family, Ownership and Employment in the family business. This three-circle model can be useful in understanding why people think or feel the way they do about certain issues surrounding the family enterprise.

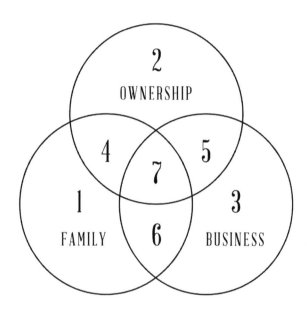

Copyright Tagiuri and Davis

It may be helpful to spend a few minutes defining each group and highlighting some of their unique questions.

l   Family members that neither work in the
     business, nor have ownership of it.

2 People that have some ownership in the business but they are
   not family members and don't actively work in the business.

3 People who are employees of the business, but
   do not have ownership and are not members
   of the family that owns the business.

4 Family members who have some ownership of the
   business but DO NOT actively work in the business.

5 People who actively work in the business and have an
   ownership stake but are NOT from the family that
   has the controlling ownership of the business.

6 Family members and employees of the business who
   DO NOT have any ownership in the business.

7 Family members that actively work in the business
   and have some ownership of the business.

WHAT DO 1'S THINK ABOUT REGARDING THE FAMILY BUSINESS?

This group is made up of family members that neither own the
business nor work in the business. For the most part this group
has opinions about the future of the business, but lack power or
influence. This group may feel a sense of nostalgia regarding the
business and may have a general desire to see the business stay in
the family to respect the heritage of their ancestors.

- Why would they change/sell the family business?
  It was a huge part of our childhood!

- Dad sold Fords, Grandpa sold Fords, Great-Grandpa
  sold Fords, why would you sell Subarus?

- How will I be able to teach my kids about what the
  business means to me if I don't own or operate it?

WHO ARE 2'S AND WHAT WORRIES THEM?

Typically 2's don't exist in most family business systems. These owners are neither family members nor employees of the business. If they do exist they are most often in the form of an investor or trustee. This group is very focused on the business as a financial asset and look at its performance from that standpoint. This group is typically not emotionally invested in the business, but they do have real questions with how it is being managed and how it is performing.

- What is the business, or this piece of it, worth?
- How much return am I getting from my investment in the business?
- Do I trust that this family will continue to manage this business profitably?
- Would it be better for me to keep this as an investment or sell it?

WHAT DO 3'S WORRY ABOUT?

Non-family employees of the business worry about what will happen to their job if the family that owns the business doesn't have a viable transition plan. They worry about family members returning to the business and limiting their opportunities or even taking their job.

- If Junior comes home from college and wants in does that mean I get the boot?
- Am I always going to be the hired hand?
- How likely is it that the family will keep the business in the family for another generation?

WHAT DO 4'S CARE ABOUT?

Individuals that are family members and have an ownership stake in the business but do not actively work in the business have some unique concerns. 4's wonder if they should be patient when the business isn't providing them with much cash flow. They are sometimes the first to second guess the management of the operation. This group often times feels like they aren't communicated with about what is happening in the business. While to everyone else it might seem "lucky" to be a non-operating owner of the family business, it has its own set of challenges.

- Is the business going to be profitable?

- Should I just wait quietly when the business is not providing much cash flow?

- Do I view the business as a community and family stewardship or just a financial asset?

- How do I feel about the management of the company?

- Do I feel informed about what is really going on in the business?

WHAT ARE THE CONCERNS OF A 5?

As a non-family owner and active participant in the business, this group has their own set of questions. The group we consider 5's worry about next generation family members coming back to the company. They sometimes wonder if they are coming back to bring value to the operation or if they are coming back because they couldn't find another job. Wondering about special treatment 5's can also question the compensation of family members that are working in the company. The biggest worry for this group is that "family issues" begin to creep in and become issues for the business.

- Are family employees talented and competent?

- Is compensation for family members that work in the business a fair market wage?

- Does the majority owner have a plan that includes making me an owner with someone I don't want to work with?

- Are family issues, like divorce or sibling rivalry, creeping in and becoming business issues?

- Do number 4's really understand the long-term value of the strategic plan?

WHAT DO 6'S THINK ABOUT?

The perceptions and challenges of a family member that is employed by the family business without any ownership are distinct. These individuals wonder what it will take to become an owner. They worry about what their parent's will says. They may even fear having to share ownership with all of their non-operating siblings and the challenges that will create. 6's also would like to know if ownership will be gifted to them or if they will need to buy the business from their parents. Sadly, some wonder if they will be, "just a hired man" for the rest of their life.

- Does dad/mom have an estate plan that includes me in the ownership of the business?

- Why does #4 get ownership of the company when they don't even work in the business?

- Why does #5 think he/she can boss me around? They aren't even apart of this family!

- Will I ever be trusted to make important decisions?
- What will it take for me to become a #7?

WHAT UNIQUE QUESTIONS DO 7'S HAVE?

The unfortunate and sometimes overwhelming challenge of the controlling owner group is that they are forced to deal with all of the questions of all of the other groups. Beyond that, they have a specific set of questions that none of the others face. Many wonder, "Does anyone care about this business as much as I do?" They also worry about how to satisfy the different needs of each of the other groups. 7's struggle with the questions that surround life after being a controlling owner. Many lack hobbies or other meaningful activities away from the business. They often simply haven't had time to develop them as the business has been their life. It can be depressing just thinking about having someone else make the day-to-day decisions about the company that they built. Finally, many struggle to figure out their cash flow needs during retirement. The questions of when to retire, how much money to expect and where it will come from are all typical challenges.

- Does anyone really care about this business or do they just want money from it?
- What would I do if I became anything else but a #7?
- Could I be happy as a #4?
- Do I believe that the next generation is prepared to inherit/operate the family business?
- Do my heirs really understand what I had to go through to build this?
- What will I do with my time if I were to step away from the company?

The three circle model isn't just an academic exercise designed to label individuals, it is actually helpful from a practical standpoint so that you can get an idea as to what the individual questions of each participant in the family business are regarding generational continuity. Take time to go through the exercise of figuring out who fits where in your family business system and identify the questions and concerns that each group might have. This will not guarantee success, but it will provide a lens through which you can better understand the nuances of the relationships regarding those that have an interest in the businesses' future.

REFLECTIONS

_____

_____

_____

_____

_____

_____

_____

_____

_____

_____

COMMITMENTS

_____

_____

_____

_____

My Little Pioneers

4

PIONEERS

Pioneer: 'to open or prepare for others to follow.'

— MERRIAM WEBSTER DICTIONARY

I n the 1840s, a group of Mormon pioneers traveled cross-country through the United States seeking safety, religious freedom, and a better life for their families and the generations who would follow.

It would be their opportunity to blaze a trail to the west and open the way for many travelers who would follow them. As we look at the patterns of the pioneers, we can learn how to perpetuate their pioneer legacy in our own time.

The pioneers who headed west were concerned about more than just getting from point A to point B. They took meticulous notes on the distances they traveled, where water was found, and dangers they encountered along the way. They dug wells from which they only drank from for a brief time; they blazed trails and cleared roads they knew they would never use again; and they planted crops they would not harvest or benefit from. Why did they do it? Why did they sacrifice their time and energy while making the journey west? What was in it for them?

Certainly, the pioneers had a vision that encompassed more than their current situation. They had a vision of paving the road for those yet to come. Such a vision produced action because they understood they were the great enablers for those who would follow. They knew that every distance recorded, every well dug, every road cleared, and every seed planted would someday benefit others who would literally follow their footsteps in the journey across the Great Plains.

Similar to the pioneers who crossed plains in the 1800s, family business owners today can be visionary pioneers who blaze the trail and prepare the way for those who follow. What vision do you have? What continuity plan does your family have in place to pave the road for those who will follow?

To truly pave the way for those who follow, important decisions must be made and crucial steps must be taken. Those who follow must know the distances to travel, where the dangers lie, and where the wells have been dug. They must be told in which fields the seeds were planted and when such fields will be ready to harvest.

All of these important elements are included in a continuity planning process. The map of the trail doesn't show distances or danger, but rather estate plans, ownership and management contingency plans. The wells are the relationships with your best customers and non-family employees, who are truly the lifeblood of your organization. The communication plan that exists between generations that provides direction and vision for the business are the planted fields waiting to be harvested.

The generations who followed the pioneers were successful because of the vision, hard work, planning, preparation, and attention to detail of the pioneers. The pioneers' path was not easy, but thousands have thanked them for their efforts that paved the way for generations of people they never knew. Have you blazed a trail in your business that is passable by generations? Are you opening the way for those who will follow? What will your pioneer legacy be?

A version of "Pioneers" first appeared in Nebraska Bankers Magazine in November 2008.

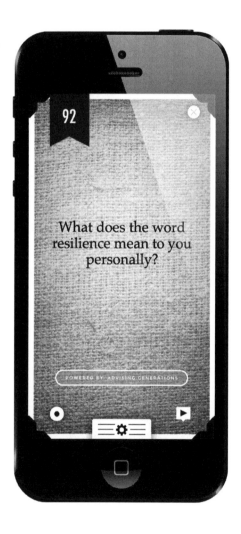

REFLECTIONS

_____

_____

_____

_____

_____

_____

_____

_____

_____

_____

COMMITMENTS

_____

_____

_____

_____

My Silly Superheroes - 2016

5

SUCCESSION SUPERHEROES

*The key to immortality is first living
a life worth remembering.*

–BRUCE LEE

F amily business leaders may have built their companies faster than a speeding bullet, but when it comes to deciding how to transition their business, many of them would prefer to hide in a phone booth.

"Faster than a speeding bullet, more powerful than a locomotive, able to leap tall buildings in a single bound. Is it a bird? Is it a plane? No, it's Superman!" The superheroes of our youth are not so far removed from our heroes now. Your favorite may have been the Incredible Hulk because of his amazing strength. Maybe it was Batman because of his gadgets and cool car. Society today often holds business owners to high expectations or places them on pedestals for their laudable characteristics such as risk-taking, tenacity in overcoming great odds and finding ways to succeed.

Family business owners are remarkable people, yet the sobering truth is that they are mortal human beings. When it comes to preparing for the inevitable -- business continuity planning -- there are four reasonably predictable ways that most business owners' attitudes can be characterized. Their thoughts and behaviors are represented here by four superheroes: Captain Immortal, Dr. Shhhh, Oblivious Man and Ms. Reality.

For the sake of simplicity, we will use three male superheroes and one female, but all the archetypes appear prevalent for female and male business owners and leaders.

CAPTAIN IMMORTAL:

He has hair that never grays, energy that never wanes and willpower seemingly stronger than life itself. The pursuit of success is both a passion and a seductress. While he is an intelligent man who at his core knows he will sometime vacate this mortal coil, he has convinced himself that day is light years away, so investing time in planning or training the next generation of superheroes is for now an irrelevant undertaking. Of course on this count, Captain Immortal lives only in the now.

DR. SHHHH:

This superhero has a plan, but he values the power and freedom of privacy more than life itself. Dr. Shhhh enjoys the seclusion he finds in developing his proprietary business solutions. He does the same thing with his hopes and dreams for the future of his family and business. He knows that he is not completely immortal, but he doesn't want anyone else to realize it. In his mind he creates plans to continue the work he has silently pursued, but refuses to share those ideas with his wife and children. He feels that this affords him a great deal of freedom. He can modify his plans as circumstances play out and never upset anyone with a midstream shift. After all, why should he have to relinquish control and information before it is absolutely necessary?

OBLIVIOUS MAN:

He is so happy doing his work that he doesn't even consider what will happen beyond his tenure, let alone consider the consequences. He goes about his superhero tasks, providing the necessities and luxuries of life for his family one day at a time. He has acquired a substantial reputation by virtue of the highly conscious manner in which he has built his business over the years. On the other hand, he has no clue that he's laying the foundation for confusion, chaos and conflicts for his family and employees by not making plans for the future of his business.

MS. REALITY:

This superhero has always been good at taking care of her business. While she enjoys the daily thrill of her work, she is highly aware that someday she will not be able to leap tall buildings in a single bound or stop an oncoming locomotive. Ms. Reality has a strong drive to succeed personally, but she has an equally keen awareness of the responsibility that she must make long-term plans for her family and business. She is just as driven to create and execute her continuity plan as she is to succeed in business because she sees planning as a critical and inevitable aspect of longer-term success.

FACING THE INEVITABLE

Just as superheroes come with different colored capes and unique abilities and powers, business owners have distinct talents and attributes that make them special. While each business owner is different, there is one thing that unites them all--mortality. Let's look inside the minds of our business-owning superhero friends.

SHAZAM! Captain Immortal refuses to face his own mortality. Business owners like him are consumed with day-to-day operations; their idea of who they are is so wrapped up in the enterprise that they can't imagine ever doing anything else. Their identity, power and sense of purpose are tied closely to the company. They struggle with making commitments to any meaningful succession planning.

KA-POW! Dr. Shhhh is slow to trust and almost impossible to communicate with. He has his ideas for what he wants to do with his business and the wealth that he has created, but he feels it is his right to withhold that information from those who will be most affected by his passing. He is reluctant to tell his children what he thinks their roles in the business should be or what they should expect from him when he passes away. He doesn't even talk to his wife about what plans he has in place for fear that she won't truly understand or will think it's "unfair" to some (or all) of the kids in the family.

One family that I consulted with was led by a man with Dr. Shhhh tendencies. The family ran a specialty auto company and dad was the founder. His son was integral to the business development and sales function of the business and his daughter was the receptionist. Mom kept the books, watched every penny and made sure the bills got paid. It was a typical small family business, until dad had a massive heart attack and died.

Dad was not a communicator and these secret tendencies became exposed as the attorney let the family know what his wishes were in his will. Dad left half the business to his wife, which wasn't a big surprise. Then the attorney let the family know that he left the other half of the business to his daughter, leaving nothing to the son. Why did he do this? Did he not trust the son? Did he want to protect his daughter? Did he assume that his wife would leave her half of the business to the son? The truth is that no one knows what his intentions were.

Fast-forward six weeks. Son comes in on a Friday afternoon and tosses his keys on the desk and announces, "I'm quitting." The following week the son opened a competing business just two streets over and essentially ran mom and sister out of business. Was that his father's intention? I doubt it, but without communication, forcing individuals into shared ownership situations without discussion can be a serious mistake.

SPLAT! Oblivious Man is so focused on running the business and taking care of his many family responsibilities that he fails to recognize the need to plan for the future. He wakes up in the morning, wipes the sleep from his eyes and then gets back to work. Almost no one will outwork him, but the well being of his family and his business are in jeopardy. With the passage of time, the jeopardy factor increases. He has good intentions, but he has not recognized the need for planning or considered the consequences for his failure to do so.

ZANG! Ms. Reality is at times the butt of her counterpart's jokes because of the meticulous manner in which she goes about planning for a successful future. She loves her work, but she fully understands that she won't be able to do it forever. With that in mind, she mentors her children who desire to join the business and encourages them to fully develop their abilities. Some of her kids aren't capable of taking on her level of leadership, and Ms. Reality is preparing to have difficult conversations with them. She also understands that not all her children will choose to enter the business; she encourages those who plan to take a different path just as enthusiastically as she supports the child she hopes will become her successor. She knows some other entrepreneurs think she doesn't have any fun, but Ms. Reality simply smiles. She sleeps well because she's done her homework and has confidence in the future. She has planned for the challenges she knows are coming.

SAVING THE SUPERHEROES FROM THEMSELVES

"Sometimes even a superhero gets into a dangerous spot and needs to be rescued." Here are some solutions to help superheroes to save themselves.

Captain Immortal: The key to rescuing Captain Immortal is to keep him from focusing on himself and get him to start focusing on immortalizing his legacy. Convincing Captain Immortal of the opportunity to have his legacy become "bullet proof" is a good first step. While he may never be convinced of his own mortality, spending effort and energy in enabling him to celebrate and perpetuate his legacy will advance the planning necessary to protect his family and his business.

Dr. Shhh: The biggest fear that Dr. Shhh has is not having his long-term plans accepted and embraced by all parties. Saving Dr. Shhh from his own secretive nature is found in his awareness of the unintended outcomes created by not being able to explain his desires and motives when he is no longer around. Dr. Shhh is concerned about keeping the peace and not creating attitudes of entitlement in the next generation. When he realizes that open communication is the best way to avoid those consequences, he will likely modify his guarded strategy.

Oblivious Man: The saving grace for Oblivious Man is his ultimate love for the business that he has created. He doesn't actively avoid planning; he just assigns a higher value to, "getting the work done." Once he takes the time to begin working "on his business" rather than always working, "in his business" the likelihood of accomplishing significant long-term planning increases dramatically.

AVOIDING THE KRYPTONITE

Which superhero do you most relate to? What is your kryptonite? All of us have conflicts between what we need and want for ourselves and for our families. We constantly battle with what's expedient and prudent, between the easier path and the harder one, between our desire to live on and on and the reality that we are mortal. The question is: Do we deny these conflicts or take them head-on? What long-term decisions should you be making for the benefit of your business and family?

A version of "Succession Planning Superheroes" first appeared in Family Business Magazine in November 2009.

REFLECTIONS

_____

_____

_____

_____

_____

_____

_____

_____

_____

_____

_____

COMMITMENTS

_____

_____

_____

_____

Symbol of Women in the Family

6

A WOMAN'S WORK-IT'S NOT WHAT YOU THINK

*The most important work you will ever do will
be within the walls of your own home.*

—HAROLD B. LEE

She is wife, mother, business partner, mediator, voice of reason, talent developer, bookkeeper, organizer, and anything else the family business needs, often covering the jobs no one else wants to do. Gloves and boots to heels and pearls are easily encompassed in a day's work. Knowing this, what, exactly, is her role in family business transitions? Women play many roles, wearing many hats, and because they do, they have the opportunity to influence generational transitions in countless way. This influence in transition planning begins when her children are very small.

WOMAN AS MOTHER

As a mother, a woman has a chance to mold and shape how her children think and feel about the family business. If Mom speaks highly of the family business, deliberately emphasizing the opportunities and benefits that it has created for the family, a child will likely grow up with a positive attitude.

If Mom complains, highlighting the challenges and painful realities of the business, children will most likely develop an aversion to being a part of the very thing everyone is working so hard to create "for them".

From a very early age a mom is planting seeds that the family will harvest when it comes time to make a transition to the next generation.

Sherry Vinton, of Chris Vinton Ranch in Nebraska is a rancher, a wife, a mother and a board member of Farm Bureau who has experienced these transitions. Sherry says of mothers, "A mother is genetically and physically hardwired to do any and everything to help that next generation succeed. I would argue that no other person is as emotionally or physically vested in the next generation's success like a mother."

WOMAN AS WIFE

As a wife, a woman also has a tremendous influence. A wife can speak to her husband in a way that no one else can. She usually knows her husbands strengths and is also well aware of his weaknesses. Her words and sometimes just her body language can influence how her husband feels about situations with the family and the farm. The commitment and sacrifices made for her husband and family to keep the business going are significant, she knows what it is like to forgo her immediate desires and embrace hard work. This puts her in a position of power. Her power to comfort, support and encourage can raise any operation to greater heights, likewise no one can belittle, destroy or weaken as a wife of the business owner can.

WOMAN AS MEDIATOR

Many times it is the woman that serves the role of mediator when the family faces parent to child transitions of ownership and management. She helps to encourage the family to have the tough conversations and is there to iron things out when the generations don't understand each other. For example: An adult ages some who works in the family business comes to mom to complain about dad's unreasonable expectations for his work schedule and about the paltry compensation package that he has to take care of his family. Mom understands the son's perspective, but is a dutiful wife and is caught in the middle of being a supportive mother and a loyal wife.

This situation is called "triangling" and is not a comfortable situation for mom to be in. Mothers are wired to fix family issues and to smooth out tense times, but in this instance the best solution is to encourage a direct dialogue between father and son so as not to get accused of choosing sides. The stress of being caught in the middle is simply unbearable for many.

Women play a significant part in family business continuity. If you are a woman and are a part of a business-owning family, embrace the power and influence that you have in these challenging times. Assume leadership in getting the dialogue started. If you are a man that has a woman in your life, allow her to guide and influence in a way that will position your family to preserve relationships and perpetuate the business. Don't underestimate the power and influence that a woman has in this crucial process.

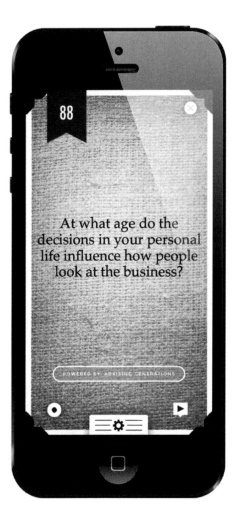

REFLECTIONS

_____

_____

_____

_____

_____

_____

_____

_____

_____

_____

_____

COMMITMENTS

_____

_____

_____

_____

Seth Green's Ewer - Succession Symbol

7

THE PARABLE OF THE EWER

PLANNING IS BRINGING THE FUTURE INTO THE PRESENT
SO THAT YOU CAN DO SOMETHING ABOUT IT NOW.

—ALAN LAKEIN

Green is a master artist, in every sense of the phrase, and his love is ceramics. Those who watch him work become mesmerized as he hovers over a potter's wheel turning clay into something beautiful or practical, it could be either, it is usually both. It's almost as if you are hearing a symphony playing as the sodden lump spins and dances its way into the shape it is intended to take.

His most recent pieces are ewers - beautiful pitchers of ancient origin formed for not just functionality but also to express the artist's creativity. When looking at a ewer - its design, form and features – the correlations with business continuity planning, especially for family businesses, begin to surface.

The ewer holds the liquid until the person who controls it wants to enjoy its contents, similar to a business as it holds the human and financial assets. The design of the container and the integrity of its walls enable the company and the ewer to receive assets and protect them from leakage, waste, spoilage or loss. Elements of a succession plan that correlate with the solid walls of the ewer are employment policies, executive compensation plans and management contingency plans.

A ewer's handle can be ornamental, but it is necessary that it be functional, strong and sturdy, allowing the liquid to be controlled in its distribution. Similarly, in a family business someone needs to have the ability to make decisions about where to take the business, how to use assets and position employees to create a successful company. One of these features might be funded by buy or sell agreements that allow for proper control by the person best suited to make those decisions. Another might be an operating agreement that stipulates how decisions about the business will be made under certain conditions.

The spout is positioned at the top of the ewer, an elegant and intelligent design, allowing for the person pouring the liquid to carefully pour from one container to another – it offers flexibility and precision to the user. The spout could represent a dividend policy that stipulates how assets can be dispersed so that there is an expectation of how dividends will be paid out. Shareholders will want to know how to access assets as needed. A well thought out structure that is communicated effectively will benefit the company and shareholders. Transparency with this policy will avoid relationship problems and allow the company to control cash flow for successful business operations.

The most interesting part of the process of building a ewer is that you don't know if it will look or function as desired until it is fired in the kiln. If material selection and construction follow correct principles, the resulting ewer is functional and beautiful; if not the pitcher will crack and be ruined in the heat.

It is much the same way that we find out how effective our business continuity plans are--the test of fire. How solid is the handle? What control do business operators have to make decisions? How sturdy is the body of the ewer? Does the business have policies and structures in place to protect the financial and human capital that the business has accumulated? How efficient is the spout? Is it clear how the senior generation will access cash from the business during their retirement years? If these can't be answered, do the hard work now before your business has a kiln-like experience.

A version of "The Parable of the Ewer" first appeared in Campden Family Business in February 2012.

REFLECTIONS

_____

_____

_____

_____

_____

_____

_____

_____

_____

_____

_____

COMMITMENTS

_____

_____

_____

_____

Papa Curtis' Cabinet Shop - Whittier, CA

8

GENERATIONAL BUSINESS 360

WE DO NOT SEE THINGS AS THEY ARE,
WE SEE THINGS AS WE ARE.

— ANAIS NIN

I n order to preserve America's most precious asset, the family business, advisors must know where gaps in perceptions exist between spouses and between generations. When beginning to work with new customers, we evaluate seven themes in the GenerationalBusiness360 process.

BUSINESS AND ESTATE PLANNING

There are a few aspects of transferring a business that make it crucial to have a solid estate plan in place. In addition to having a plan that incorporates strategies to minimize taxes and facilitate an orderly transfer of assets, a good estate plan should also account for the management and ownership needs that may exist within the family business.

The best plans are developed when a team of professionals including a CPA, an attorney, an insurance professional, a wealth manager and a banker work together with a family to develop a plan. This strategy ensures a plan that not only accomplishes the business needs but also provides for the needs of the family.

Tax laws and family needs are always changing, so a good estate plan should also provide a level of flexibility that allows the plan to adapt over time. Individuals should reanalyze their estate plans periodically and make necessary adjustments as circumstances require. Performing a periodic review of an estate plan may also help identify additional planning opportunities where business interests may be transferred in the most economical manner.

COMMUNICATION

Communication of intentions and dreams of both the senior generation and the next generation is crucial, but that can sometimes be difficult. However, the ability to work through challenges while speaking respectfully is crucial to the success of any family business. Families that set aside time to discuss the business and the goals for the family will increase their likelihood for success.

LEADERSHIP DEVELOPMENT

Grooming family members in the next generation to run a business takes both initiative and patience. An intentional skill development plan will give them the necessary abilities and confidence to allow the senior generation to delegate meaningful responsibility when the time is right. Creating expectations and accountability will aid them in their growth.

TRUST

There are many types of trust that need to be in place for a generational transfer to be successful. Members of the senior generation must trust the decision-making ability of the next generation in both personal and business life. They must also trust that the younger family members have similar goals for the future of the business.

Equally important is the next generation's level of trust in the senior generation regarding intentions for the future. If either side doesn't trust the other, the process of transitioning the business will most likely break down.

PERSONAL RESILIENCE

Just as personal resilience is one of the elements that make a business successful to begin with, it is also essential for the continued success of a business. Effective business owners know how to learn from their mistakes, embrace change, and do not give up when things are difficult. If the next generation doesn't have a great deal of personal resilience, things might not go as expected.

It's best to find out early if someone intended to take over the business isn't wired to be an owner. If this is the case, more focus must be placed on developing a support network to help the future owner successfully manage the business.

RETIREMENT AND INVESTMENT PLANNING

Most successful family business owners have one common challenge—they are usually asset rich but relatively cash poor. When considering the prospect of transitioning out of the operation, the senior generation's retirement cash flow sources and needs should be carefully planned for. It should be determined what the desire for cash flow is, and that expectation should be measured against the ability of the business to create it. Families who want business continuity through the generations would be wise to do everything they can to create alternative sources of retirement cash flow.

KEY NON-FAMILY EMPLOYEES

In family business succession, key nonfamily employees are sometimes the most important piece of the puzzle. Taking the opportunity to share the family's visions and dreams for the future with key employees can instill confidence and loyalty in a group that will ultimately help navigate the business through the most difficult part of the transition. Sometimes communicating with key employees is enough, but other times financial incentives are used to entice them to help the family make the transition successfully.

Each family has unique issues in its generational transfer situations. But when you identify the strengths, weaknesses, and gaps in perception with the seven themes of the GenerationalBusiness360™

process, you will increase the likelihood for success exponentially. Focusing on working through these challenges with customers is the most important step you can take in helping to preserve America's most precious asset, the family business.

A version of "GenerationalBusiness360" first appeared in The Edge Magazine in May 2012.

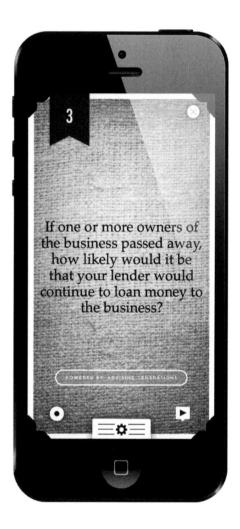

REFLECTIONS

_____

_____

_____

_____

_____

_____

_____

_____

_____

_____

COMMITMENTS

_____

_____

_____

_____

Early Days @ Duncan Aviation

9

BUSINESS TRANSITIONS AND THE PLANE ANALOGY

*Perspective is the way we see things when we
look at them from a certain distance, and it
allows us to appreciate their true value.*

—RAFAEL E PINO

I t's like a dream. No massive smelly parking garages, no interminable lines, no overworked airline agents or glassy-eyed security violating your personal space, in fact, you are able to simply walk straight from your car to the airplane. Not a dream, nor a time warp, simply your first flight on a private plane.

Boarding is wonderfully simple, refreshing, it is just you and the pilot. He hands you a headset to muffle the noise, which will be much more significant here than on a commercial flight, and allow for personal communication throughout the trip. New to this mode of travel the unexpected roar of the engines is a little unnerving, the headset allows you to relax and feel a little more at ease as you hear the pilot communicating with air traffic control.

As you prepare for takeoff, the air is filled with excitement, adrenaline and maybe even a little fear. You aren't sure exactly what to expect, but the thrill of getting off the ground and into the air in such a small craft has your heart racing in anticipation. As you make your way to the runway and power up for takeoff, the experienced pilot holds the controls steady as the plane jostles from left to right. Not only is the sound of the engine much more pronounced, so is every movement of the plane, every bump in the seemingly smooth runway. A little unsure at this point, you steal a glance at the pilot, his calm confident expression reassures you that everything is proceeding normally and bolsters your trust. You are along for the ride. The noise, the shaking and rattling increase to a climactic pitch then abruptly cease, as you lift off the ground and begin to hum your gradual ascent into the sky. As the ground falls away beneath you it seems to take your anxiety with it, your breath begins to slow and a sense of calm and wonder overtakes you as you climb into the gray beyond.

Just about the time you are getting comfortable, you enter thick, dark clouds. Sure, you've flown through clouds before on 747s, but, when you are in a small plane sitting right next to the pilot, it is obvious that visibility is an issue. You are flying strictly by your instruments. Your body once again begins to tense as you realize this is what they call "flying blind". It seems as though you are forever engulfed in the gray abyss of the clouds.

Eventually the clouds begin to dissipate and visibility comes and goes, as you continue climbing— eventually you break through. You exhale a long and steady breath as your body responds and relaxes. You are now above the clouds and the sky is perfectly clear.

Enjoying this newfound clarity, you notice that you are "above the world", not even able to see the earth beneath you because of the blanket of clouds below. It's peaceful, yet, lonely. You can't even see any other planes.

And then, before you really tire of the quiet solitude, it's time to descend and prepare for landing. Once again you enter the ominous clouds, fly by your instruments and wait for "break through", when you can once again see the ground and actually get a visual on where you are supposed to land. The plane approaches the runway, lines up, adjusting speed accordingly and with a squeal of rubber on asphalt, touches safely down. On slightly trembling legs, you now begin to consider all of the feelings you've just had during the flight and realize that you were the only one experiencing those feelings. The rest of the world has no idea of your journey—the multitude of thoughts and feelings. The rest of the world just knows that a flight has landed and they're ready for you to deplane and get to work. Not even the pilot can truly appreciate the passenger experience.

This journey is much the same way with a next generation leader transitioning into a significant leadership role in the family company.

We begin again at the airport, where the next generation decides they want to fly. Next generation leaders many times don't face the same "waiting lines" or "Transportation Security Agent" treatment that non-family leaders might. Many times these individuals literally walk straight into the company. While this may seem like the easy way, we all know that next generation leaders will forever be held to a higher standard by their peers at work because they bypassed typical "lines and the security checkpoints."

When the next generation leader figuratively "boards the plane" he or she is usually sitting next to mom or dad who is experienced and competent. There is more noise and chaos than sometimes expected and hopefully the senior generation has the foresight to recognize the need for "headsets" to drown out noise and to allow for communication during the journey. These headsets may come in the form of individual mentoring sessions or family meetings facilitated by the practitioner, to discuss the business, the family and the journey. The more the family can do to keep communication lines open during the leadership transition journey, the better.

As the business welcomes next generation leadership, there is a sense of excitement and anticipation for the journey. "The takeoff" is filled with adrenaline and some insecurity. The senior generation maintains the controls and leads the effort of keeping the business straight during acceleration and takeoff. This is not the time to turn over the controls. It should be understood that nerves and uncertainty at this stage are normal, especially for the next generation.

A successful take-off is often quickly followed by a new set of challenges soon as the plane enters the clouds, losing visibility, the senior generation needs to communicate and demonstrate that they know how to use the instruments to navigate through impaired vision. This is probably a good time for the senior generation to teach what some of the instruments mean and how they work.

Sometimes when the business transition is "in the clouds" and lacks a perceptible end goal, it can become stressful to the less experienced passenger. Take for example a situation with a disgruntled employee or a touchy media issue regarding the industry that you work in. It is in these times the senior generation's experience can have a steadying influence to guide and mentor the next generation and the company through the difficult situation.

Breaking through the clouds figuratively is a time where the business has navigated through some uncertainty where both generations were involved. A sense of clarity and peace stretches out in the journey ahead. However, just as in our analogy, it can seem pretty lonely flying above the clouds. It can cause the next generation to lose perspective of their positioning and relationship with the ground. One way this occurs is when the next generation ascends too quickly in leadership and doesn't have relationships with the frontline employees or understand the key aspects of what makes the business successful.

Finally, as the flight is coming to an end and the pilot descends to the earth, the pilot and passenger must re-enter the clouds of uncertainty to get to the ground once again. Passing through clouds and seeing the ground, the pilot must align him or herself with the runway, adjust speed accordingly and position for a safe and smooth landing. The same is true in a business transition. The senior generation is ultimately responsible for the success of this landing, which is accomplished when great care is taken for positioning the plane for the runway and observing the weather conditions that are all around you. In business it is crucial for the senior generation to have a plan for their cash flow during retirement. It is also imperative to give the next generation a clear indication of when they would like to retire so that they can gauge how long they have to develop the necessary skills to take the controls.

The culminating observation, once you are safely on the ground, is that the rest of the world doesn't know (or perhaps even care) about this journey—it's stress and uncertainty. The rest of the world wants the next generation to hit the ground running and to do the work that needs to be done. Is it fair? Maybe not. Does it matter? Absolutely not! The opportunities that you have that others do not will make you a target for unfair expectations. Fair or not, this is what you should expect.

The journey that each multi-generational family business takes during transition is unique. There will be excitement and there are sure to be times of uncertainty. It may be full of excitement or it may instill fear. The key is to approach the journey by preparing both generations to execute the flight plan. Pack well, pack early, enjoy the journey and expect that there will be turbulence along the way!

A version of "A Plane - Business Transition and the Private Plan Analogy" first appeared in The Practitioner in October 2012.

REFLECTIONS

_____

_____

_____

_____

_____

_____

_____

_____

_____

_____

_____

COMMITMENTS

_____

_____

_____

_____

Abel Construction – Building Nebraska

10 THINGS TO CONSIDER BEFORE
JOINING THE FAMILY BUSINESS

1 What your salary will be before moving your wife and 5 kids. Dad probably said something like this. "There's plenty of work to do. Come on home and we'll figure it out."

2 That you may spend 25 years building the family business only to learn that you have to share ownership with all of your siblings, none of whom work in the business.

3 That your dad may live to age 100 and that you may actually inherit the business 15 years AFTER you retire.

4 That you will probably be compared to your father and never really be able to live outside his shadow.

5 That your family may have the "opportunity" to repurchase your own business thanks to a lack of estate tax planning and Uncle Sam wanting his portion at your parent's death. This is when you think, "Dad, I guess we should have listened to that life insurance salesman after all."

6 That part of your "inheritance" may require you to personally guarantee all of the debts of the family business. "Boy is your spouse going to be excited to hear this!" Not.

7 That you may have to cut a check each year to your cousins that you've never actually met because Uncle John gifted them stock. "And you will probably do it with a smile and

not even a hint of animosity!" (Insert forced smile here.)

8 That everyone in town may assume that everything
   that you've ever achieved was simply handed to you.
   You've even been referred to as being a member of
   the "lucky lineage club" or something like that.

9 That you may be on every community fundraiser's
   call list and have to feel guilty for only helping
   some charities. "You never thought that you would
   feel guilty for giving, but sadly, you will."

10 That by joining the family business you may miss
   the chance to do work you don't care about and may
   not have the opportunity to make some heartless
   corporation lots of money. "You may feel like you were
   robbed of the experience that most men and women
   have in the work force." Joining the family business
   isn't for everyone. Go in with your eyes wide open!

Jhett's Heavy Load

10

UNINTENDED CONSEQUENCES OF SHARED OWNERSHIP

Receiving is good but giving is much better.
Nevertheless, sharing is the best.

—SHAHRIZAD SHAFIAN

E veryone loves the family business, the independence, the flexibility, continuing a family legacy and so on. All that is true until you have to share ownership and make operating decisions with a non-operating sibling. Choosing to come back and work in the business represents an opportunity for independence and an avenue to avoid the corporate bureaucracy that many of your friends have to deal with in their jobs. Then it happens, mom or dad passes away and you learn their estate plan calls for you to share ownership with your sister who has an office job in Chicago.

While, from your parents' perspective, this seems like the logical and fair way to transition ownership, it introduces a new complexity into your life. Shared ownership is the toughest thing that you can ask a human being to do, especially with a farming operation. If you think back to when you were a kid, imagine having to share ownership in a car with your not-so caring brother. You may have different ideas about mechanical maintenance. You may not share the same standards of cleanliness and overall upkeep. One of you may seem to always leave the gas tank mostly empty. All of these differences can lead to conflict and may even be detrimental to the long-term value of the car.

Sharing ownership in a farm or business is even more complex. Share ownership may entail decisions about equipment purchases, land use, marketing decisions and financing needs. These are all critical for the long-term health of the business and reaching consensus on each of these items is essential. While it is likely that all siblings love the business, it is not likely that all share the same perspective on these issues.

One family that I consulted with wanted to attempt a shared ownership arrangement between brothers where one of them had engaged in an inappropriate relationship with the other brother's wife years earlier. The family knew about the indiscretion yet continued to think that shared ownership was the best way to set up their estate plan.

After consultation with the family, it became clear that shared ownership would not be beneficial for either couple and would not be good for the business either. An alternative arrangement was made.

If shared ownership is the path for your family, it will be important for each party to know their rights and accept their roles. It is also important for each family to have a way for members of the family to sell their interest in the business in a way that gives the business an opportunity to maintain its family ownership, while providing a fair price for the family member that wants out.

Transparency and a communicated plan for how families can unwind these sibling ownership structures is crucial to preserving relationships and perpetuating the business operation across generations. Shared ownership can be emotionally challenging and can make the best communicators feel a little uneasy. The last thing you want is to have family members feel they are being held hostage by the family business.

Here are three ways to minimize risk with shared ownership relationships.

1   Create a clear understanding of the rights and obligations of ownership in the business for operators and non-operators.

2   Develop a consistent and structured pattern of communication around central issues relating to the long-term success of the operation. (Example: Semi-annual meetings to update non-operating family members)

3   Avoid shared ownership obligations when family members vary significantly in the areas of risk taking and personality differences.

While it seems the goal of every parent is to treat their children fairly and with love, shared ownership in the business operation isn't always the best way to communicate that feeling. Take time to understand the true challenges with forcing your children into a shared ownership situation and then put together a plan and communicate your intentions for the business and for the family. Shared ownership may work well for many, but make sure that you are going into it with your eyes wide open.

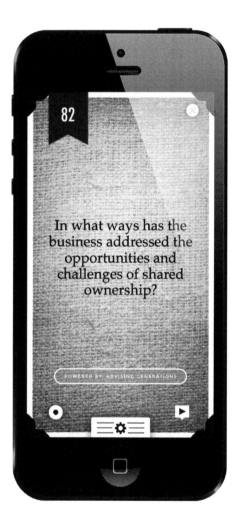

REFLECTIONS

COMMITMENTS

Mind Your Business

11

THEFT IN THE FAMILY BUSINESS...IS IT HAPPENING TO YOU?

Thou shalt not steal.

—EXODUS 20:15

I t all started when a daughter working in her father's business found herself taking money that she had not earned. Over a two-year period things steadily declined from bad to worse, in the end the stolen money was well into the six-figure range.

The family's CPA was the one that detected the abnormality. The most severe problems arose when the IRS gave the business owner an ultimatum: "Pay the tax or we will criminally prosecute your daughter."

The owner loved his daughter, but he knew that bailing her out would ultimately be to her detriment and he didn't have the money to pay the IRS, so he allowed the prosecution to go forward. Heartbroken for his daughter and worried about his business, he watched as his daughter was convicted of a felony. She was given years of probation and was ordered restitution of all the funds.

The crazy twist of events didn't end at that point. The terrible irony came in that because the daughter then had a felony on her record she was unable to obtain a job, and so she ultimately found herself again working for her father in the same company she originally stole from.

Corporate scandals, embezzlement of funds, front-page headlines about theft only happen in large corporations, right? It is believed that these large, faceless corporations are the businesses that are most vulnerable to theft. This may be true, but could these things happen in your family business? The answer is yes.

Sadly, theft is more likely to happen in a family business where there is a higher level of trust and more responsibility given to fewer people — an environment where there are fewer formalities and structures in place to safeguard the companies' assets.

"There are two keys to keeping your business from being stolen from. First is to have a system for prevention, and second is to have a system for detection," said Tom Grafton, a CPA from Lincoln, NE, and expert in the field.

WHY DO PEOPLE STEAL?

To understand the problem of theft, you must first enter the mind of someone who steals. It isn't always the person you see on the street corner who has a menacing look that is most likely to steal from your small company. Often the more likely perpetrator is someone who looks more middle-class, less threatening. Someone close to you, whom you feel you know and has your confidence, who may even have the same nose or chin that you do. Are you following me? Yes, a family member.

People steal for many reasons. The main reason people steal is that they feel justified because of a specific impending need. It is often rationalized as something temporary, with the thought that they will put the money back when they were done "borrowing" it. The problem is that the money usually does not find its way back to the company.

Another reason people might steal is because they have uncontrolled access to funds or assets. The temptation of having access to money and the awareness that no one would know if some got "lost" is simply too much temptation for some people to overcome.

A third reason people steal is because of personal pressures. They may have a debt that is coming due. They may have an addiction to drugs, alcohol or shopping that they need to satisfy. They may be in an abusive relationship, and they see the money as a way out. Exploring the motivations and avenues of theft would take an entire book to analyze so it is best to simply be aware of how real and how close this problem is.

HOW VULNERABLE IS YOUR BUSINESS?

There are several ways in which your business might be susceptible to theft. The first way is if there are lone people in the organization that handle money and exchanges without a second set of eyes to check those transactions. Having multiple people who count money before making deposits will not only protect the business from thieves, it also protects the employees from undue temptation and also false accusation if at some time the money doesn't add up. Trusting one person to handle the finances in a family business is a mistake that is often paid for in larceny.

How do you protect against theft?

Grafton shares that there are four things you can do to prevent theft in the family business and three major activities to detect theft when it does happen.

PREVENTION:

- Limit physical access to blank check stock and account for all checks utilized.

- Limit authorized signature to the bank account.

- Limit access to business debit/credit cards.

- Perform background checks on potential hires.

DETECTION:

- Produce monthly financial statements and scan for unusual balances.

- Review or perform monthly bank reconciliations to assure accurate preparation and validity of reconciling items.

- Receive (unopened) bank and credit card statements each month and review for reasonableness, unknown or unusual activities.

Be aware that the reasons people steal are varied. Be vigilant in knowing your employees and their personal challenges. Talk about the responsibility for each employee to be a steward of the assets they are charged to look over. Protect them from their own weaknesses by putting in systems of checks and balances that help them to avoid unnecessary temptation.

Don't let your family business fall victim to the unfortunate event of theft. Prepare your people, put the systems in place to prevent and detect theft, and then move forward with confidence.

REFLECTIONS

_____

_____

_____

_____

_____

_____

_____

_____

_____

_____

_____

COMMITMENTS

_____

_____

_____

_____

Me, Grandma Gibbons and Dr. Seuss

12

THE QUIET KILLER OF THE FAMILY BUSINESS

---

*Out of all the things I've lost,
I miss my mind the most.*

−MARK TWAIN

What is the biggest risk to the generational transition of the family business? Is it estate taxes, generational communication, market challenges, rising interest rates or is it something else?

While all of these issues are threats to the family business, they may not be the toughest to deal with. The quiet killer of the family business is the potential for long-term care needs for the senior generation. With medical advances, American's life expectancies continue to extend, and while this is good in many ways, it can also increase the costs incurred towards the final years of someone's life.

Many business owners spend time transitioning management duties, finding ways to tax efficiently and passing on the ownership of the enterprise, but not enough time is spent working through the risk of long term care events. The financial strain of having a family member need long-term care is sometimes too much for the business to bear.

Maria Sarci, a Long Term Care expert from New Jersey, sees some common misconceptions around long-term care. She shares four typical fallacies that are commonly accepted.

1 "I won't ever need Long-Term Care."

According to the US Department of Health and Human Services statistics show that 70% of individuals over the age of 65 will experience a care event.

2 "My family will provide the care for me."

While families have the best intentions, physical limitations, house layout or the inability of a caregiver to modify or give up their own job to care for the individual often limits the family's ability to provide such care. Medical expertise and experience also become an issue with many individuals that need this type of care.

3 "I'll pay for it out of pocket."

Depending on the level of care necessary, the costs can be tough for a business to cash flow. According to the Genworth 2014 Cost of Care Study, the average cost of "hands-off care" like cooking, cleaning and running errands is averaging $19 per hour. If your needs require you to be in an assisted living facility, the national median monthly rate is $3,500 per month, with those costs rising steadily every year.

If a loved one requires a private room in a nursing home care facility the national median daily rate is $240, which adds up to over $87,000 per year.

4 "I will be covered by Medicare or Medicaid."

Sarci also explains, "Medicare is limited to those that are 65 or older and typically is limited to 100 days of care and the costs are capped." She also shares, "Medicaid is designed for the impoverished and significantly limits the type of care that you can receive. The choices around the type of facility and environment you live in become a decision of the government, not the family."

As you consider planning for the risk of having a long-term care need, be aware of the myths and truths that surround the options and plan accordingly.

Communicate with family about their intentions to care for family members in home or if full-time care will be considered. Families should also calculate the potential cost of care and determine if the business can provide the necessary cash flow to cover a long-term care event. As you consider these questions, it should help your family decide how to deal with the risk of long-term care for your senior generation. Don't let the silent killer of the family business end your legacy; plan accordingly.

A version of "The Quiet Killer of the Family Business" first appeared in Successful Farming Magazine in September 2014. Meredith Corporation. All Rights Reserved.

63

Describe the ability of the business to financially cope with one of the owners having to enter Long Term Care.

POWERED BY: ADVISING GENERATIONS

REFLECTIONS

_____

_____

_____

_____

_____

_____

_____

_____

_____

_____

_____

COMMITMENTS

_____

_____

_____

_____

Libby's Favorite Treats

13

SUCKER-COMMUNICATION AND THE DUM DUM PARADOX

Speak clearly if you speak at all;
carve every word before you let it fall.

—OLIVER WENDELL HOLMES, SR.

"No, there wasn't a bunch of kinds of candy. There was just suckers."

"Yes there was! I sawed them, there was whole bunches of kinds."

I sighed as I listened to my children arguing in the back seat. It was a beautiful, warm Sunday afternoon, we were just on our way home from church, and we were already in a fight. I listened more closely to learn the root of the problem and what I heard I now call the Dum Dums™ Paradox.

My six-year old daughter was trying to explain to my four-year-old son that the person who had been handing out candy at the end of the meeting only had one kind, Dum Dums. In her mind it was clear that the candy jar contained only one kind of treat. The four-year-old, however, was trying to get her to recognize that there were many different flavors of candy in the jar. Neither understood the other, but both were convinced that they were right.

As I listened, I knew what each of them meant and their intent to explain it to the other, but there was an obvious disconnect. As their voices and frustration elevated, I was not optimistic about how this would end. After letting my children's argument play out for some time to see if they could come to an understanding on their own, I intervened.

I explained to my daughter that when her brother said that there were different kinds of candy, he really meant flavors. To my son I clarified that all of the candies in the jar were called Dum Dums, or suckers, but that there were cherry suckers and orange suckers and chocolate suckers. Gradually understanding began to dawn and cooler heads prevailed.

How often do we get caught living out the Dum Dum Paradox? How often do we seek to be heard and understood before we seek to listen and understand? To avoid the Dum Dum Paradox in our lives we have to make a sincere effort to listen and understand what others mean, not just words that are coming out of their mouths. In families, opportunities for misunderstanding abound. In a family business this is amplified many times over, with misinterpretations between generations being the most common.

It is crucial for family business members to first seek to understand rather than be understood. Here are three remedies to keep your family from living out the Dum Dum Paradox:

| "Seek to understand others before you seek to be

understood." (As Stephen R. Covey so eloquently explained)

2 Remember the 2:1 ratio of ears to mouth. The ability to listen twice as much as we speak is truly a refined art. Replace a portion of your talking with an added measure of listening.

3 Keep perspective. Don't make minor issues major. Life will allow for plenty of experiences with major issues; we don't need to create them.

Learning these remedies is crucial to effective communications with family and co-workers. Don't fall victim to the Dum Dum Paradox. That's for suckers!

A version of "Sucker- Lessons in Communication" first appeared in Nebraska Bankers Magazine in August 2010.

REFLECTIONS

_____

_____

_____

_____

_____

_____

_____

_____

_____

_____

COMMITMENTS

_____

_____

_____

_____

Cash, Cars + IOUs

14

THE COMPENSATION CONUNDRUM

*Do your job and demand your
compensation-but in that order.*

−CARY GRANT

"Dad, we need to have a talk about my salary. I think I should be paid more for the work I do."

"Son, when I was your age I didn't take a paycheck for six months to get this business started, and then when it got going I paid myself as little as possible to be able to grow the business."

Sound familiar? If it does, you are not alone. In family businesses there is an evolution that may include wondering if the operation will make it to feeling confident in the long-term viability of the business. As the business matures, it is important to go from informal to more structured processes and procedures.

Compensation is one of those areas that need to be discussed openly and regularly, thus allowing the evolution to take place over time.

STAGES OF THE FAMILY BUSINESS

Every family business starts as an entrepreneurial organization that may have one employee/owner and a dream. If the business survives the entrepreneurial phase, employees are added, business structure and processes are introduced. As the business grows beyond the founder, job descriptions are developed, non-family employees are hired and compensation is determined based on the competitive landscape of the marketplace.

If the business continues to grow and talented employees that are key to the ongoing success of the business are recognized as valuable assets, compensation packages are developed to incentivize employee loyalty and to continue growth within the company. This progression happens in family businesses just like in any other organization, except it is not always the same for family members that work in the business.

The experience of the founder and the memory of when things were tight doesn't fade fast and so when the next generation comes back and expects to be paid a market wage for the job they perform, there is sometimes a disconnect. The resulting perception may be that the senior generation is being "unfair" or too tight with the purse strings, while the next generation is accused of wanting too much, too fast. While both of these explanations may be true in some situations, they are not true in all cases.

The senior generation expects the next generation to make similar sacrifices as they did, because that is what made them successful.

The next generation feels the need to be treated fairly from a salary perspective because they are many times not positioned to "win" in the same way as their parents when the company is successful. The next generation doesn't necessarily benefit financially when the company's equity grows. Ownership is sometimes slow to come, and so there is strain between the compensation package and the ultimate ownership strategy of the senior generation.

Perhaps this example is a generalization but it illustrates the need to visit compensation often; at least as frequently as one would expect in a more corporate setting.

WHAT IS YOUR TRUE COMPENSATION PACKAGE?

To begin this conversation, both generations should have a clear understanding of what the true compensation package is. For example, in agriculture it is sometimes the case that housing, utilities and even the use of acreage is made available to the next generation without paying market value or sometimes any rent at all. If this is the case, it should be considered part of the compensation package. If vehicles, fuel, insurance or other benefits are a part of the package, they should also be included in the discussion. It is important that both generations recognize what the other considers part of the compensation package.

Consider the following scenario. Son complains to his friend that he is only paid a $2,000 per month wage for working on the family ranch and he puts in 60-70 hours per week and is expected to not take vacations or time away. In the same case the father may complain to his buddies that his son doesn't appreciate the rich compensation package that his son has. "We pay for his housing, electricity, water, his pickup and fuel, his kids have horses that we feed and we still pay him $2,000 per month, and he still doesn't think it's enough."

Both generations should work to understand the needs and perspectives of the other and discuss what will work for them as well as what they value. The next generation needs to take into consideration the lifestyle and benefits that they have and use fair comparisons when they look at the compensation of their peers.

The compensation conversation is always a tough one. The balance of being competitive with pay, while assuring that the company is viable is a challenge. The reality of the senior generation's "true" compensation package should also be considered. Did they really just pay themselves a measly salary with no upside when the company performed well? If the next generation isn't participating in the upside of when the business is profitable, should their pay really be compared to what the senior generation's pay was when they started in the business?

HOW MUCH IS TOO MUCH?

There is a spectrum when business-owning families face compensation. One extreme is not paying family members enough for the role they fulfill; the other is paying them too much.

Family wealth advisor Paul Comstock, from Houston, Texas, cautions families to "pay a market wage for the job description that is outlined. It shouldn't matter if the role is filled by a family member or not, the role should be paid at market wage." Paul warns about the conflicts that arise from not compensating according to the specific role the family member fills.

Here are three possible challenges that Comstock sees in working with business-owning families regarding compensation.

1 The next generation knows they are getting paid more than they deserve for the role they fulfill. As much as they might like the extra income, this will actually hurt their confidence in the long run and skew their sense of what their work is worth.

2 The non-family employees who are peers will come to resent the family member that is treated better than they are for doing the same thing.

3 The business begins to be treated less like a competitive enterprise and more like a family piggy bank, leading to the ultimate downfall of the company.

These are challenges for each business-owning family to confront. The fairest compensation package is the one that is discussed in "apples to apples" terms in a respectful and open manner. When the generations appreciate the contributions of each other and when both are focused on adding more value to the business than their compensation package warrants is when success and harmony are found.

Avoid the compensation conundrum by facing these issues head on and putting a plan together that is fair, competitive and communicated.

A version of "The Compensation Conundrum" first appeared in Successful Farming Magazine in December 2013. Meredith Corporation. All Rights Reserved.

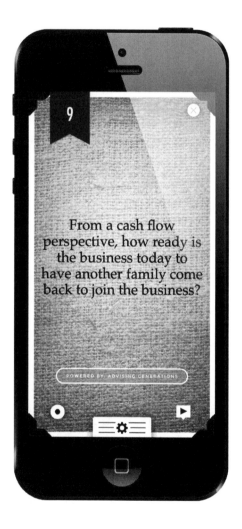

REFLECTIONS

_____

_____

_____

_____

_____

_____

_____

_____

_____

_____

_____

COMMITMENTS

_____

_____

_____

_____

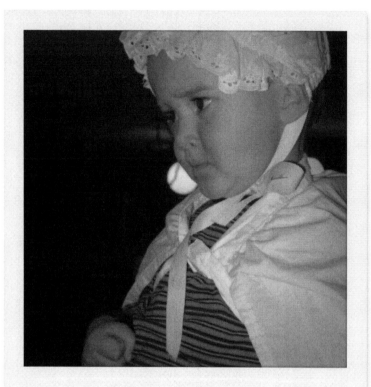

Nativity Scene Gone Wrong - 2008

15

'I AM NOT A SHEEP!'- THE CHALLENGES OF FITTING IN

*Conformity is the jailer of freedom
and the enemy of growth.*

—JOHN F. KENNEDY

I t's Christmas Eve at grandma's house, the extended family has gathered and is preparing to re-enact the Nativity. Little girls fight over who will be the gentle Mary, and in-laws draw straws for the role of the donkey. My 2-year-old son walks into the room with a white apron tied on backwards and a white ruffled lace bonnet. He had obviously been dressed by one of his young aunts to be a makeshift sheep. The only problem was that he wasn't buying the idea.

I remark that he makes a very nice looking sheep, he quickly turns to me with a fierce scowl, and in his little gruff voice shouts, "I am not a sheep, I'm a superhero!"

In that moment I realize that while the family has an idea of how my son should fit into the story, he is not seeing it. He went along with their attempts long enough to get a costume, but that was it. How many times does this happen in a family business?

One example of this challenge took place with one of my favorite students at The University of Nebraska. After the first day of class Betsy came up to me after class and confessed to me that she had no intention of returning to the family business and the only reason she was taking the class was because her father basically told her she needed to. At that point she was looking for me to tell her that she shouldn't take the class, but I didn't let her off that easy.

The business that her family owns is called Speedway Motors and it is known throughout the United States as "America's Oldest Speed Shop." She explained to me that she didn't have a natural interest in dirt track racing and didn't see herself fitting in the male dominated sport. Fast forward just six months and Betsy discovered that her passion for social media and marketing was one way that she could carve out a niche and add real value to Speedway Motors. In just a couple of years she built the online division and social media platforms into a growing and thriving business itself.

At times, parents in pride and anticipation tell their kids, "Someday you will own this business." And I just picture my disgruntled son saying, "I am not a sheep, I am a superhero."

Do business owners ever consider the fact that their dream might not be their child's? In Betsy's case she had to discover that her talents and passion could be applied to the family business. Do parents listen to their children enough to know what they really should be encouraging them to pursue?

A family can have the most profitable hot dog factory in the state or the most successful car dealership in the country, but does the next generation have enough of a passion for hot dogs or automobiles to carry the torch? Multi-generational success in business happens when multiple generations are passionate about the same business. Cash flow and profitability aside, a genuine interest and love for the business is essential for successful family business continuity.

How do you develop in and encourage your children to discover their passion? No one wants to watch someone they love grind away at a job they despise simply out of a sense of duty. Nor is that the best scenario for business productivity or happy family relations. Luckily, in the world we live in there is no limit to the opportunities for creating job niches that are customized to maximize talent and utilize training where there is desire and a willingness to work hard.

Here are five tips followed by a deeper exploration of each:

1 Always speak positively about the business

2 Bring children along as much as
   possible when they are young

3 Have other trusted employees work with
   your children as they are developing

4 Expose children to different aspects of the
   business and see how they respond

5 Talk about what owning a business allows you
   to do for the community and the family

Speaking positively about the business is one of the easiest things a parent can do to create goodwill in the mind of a child. Frequent complaining about the business will surely discourage potential future business owners from wanting to carry on the family enterprise. Beware of planting the seeds of criticism. "We reap what we sow." The old saying, "If you don't have anything nice to say, don't say anything at all," has real application if your intent is to attract your posterity to someday join the family business.

Including children at an early age is usually a very positive experience for them and will create memories that link them to the business. Angie Muhleisen, President of Union Bank and Trust in Lincoln, NE agrees saying, "I grew up hearing my father talk about banking around the family dinner table. Even though I didn't realize it at the time, these conversations taught me a lot about banking and were the catalyst for my life-long interest in the profession." Being proud of the business and allowing children to be around as much as possible builds ties to the business that someday might be strong enough to make them want to come back to join and lead.

It is a wise investment to allow children to experience the business and what goes on there, while not always under the watchful eye of mom or dad is important. Family Business thought leader and Professor at Brigham Young University, Gibb Dyer explains, "I have found that finding a nonfamily mentor for family members to be extremely valuable in helping them develop their talents and get the feedback they need to grow and improve." Supporting a trusted employee and encouraging them to mentor and befriend them may be the difference between pushing children away from the family business and encouraging them to gravitate back towards it.

Exposing the next generation to many aspects of the business is important for a couple of reasons. First, it gives children an opportunity to learn what they like most about the business and what they enjoy least. It also gives the senior generation a chance to see the next generation's natural talent or inclinations to certain areas of the business. Finding the right fit in the company is key to retaining and inspiring the next generation to stay with the firm and grow in their leadership abilities.

Lastly, it is important to not only talk about the business itself, but to talk about the benefits and opportunities that business ownership provides for you individually and for the family. Speak of the importance of the business in the community and share the charitable and civic opportunities that you have had as a business owner. Express your gratitude about the benefits of owning a business, especially those that seem unrelated, or are not always clearly visible to the next generation.

Remember, when you are growing your business and introducing the next generation to it, don't assume that just because you've got them in the apron and bonnet that they will want to be a sheep. The last thing that you want is for a child to join the business and then have them tell you, "I am not a sheep, I am a superhero." Encourage, train, and mentor them if that is their inclination, but let it be their passion. Ask "Inspired Questions" along the way to help then navigate their talents, then the family business will have a good chance to survive and even thrive for multiple generations.

A version of "I am not a sheep" originally appeared in Nebraska Bankers Magazine in January 2011.

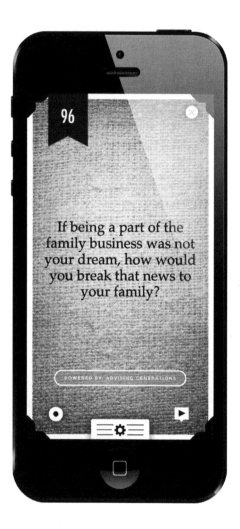

REFLECTIONS

_____

_____

_____

_____

_____

_____

_____

_____

_____

_____

_____

COMMITMENTS

_____

_____

_____

_____

3 Generations of Flying

16

PREPARING FOR TAKEOFF

When everything seems to be going against you, remember that the airplane takes off into the wind, not with it.

—HENRY FORD

The cabin lights dim while the growl of the engines deepens, the G forces of powerful acceleration press you back into your seat and your heart skips a few beats while the airplane noses upward into the sky and off the ground. While on a recent trip I began to analyze the many similarities between a pilot flying a plane and a next-generation business leader taking on meaningful responsibility in the family firm. While it's exciting to be on an airplane as it accelerates into its takeoff, I've been told that it is one of the most dangerous parts of flying. Similarly, the way a next-generation member assumes meaningful responsibility in a family firm has implications for the future leader's long-term success in the organization.

As I observed the airplanes taking off, five specific parallels became clear.

1 Rigorous training and preparation are required.

Just as a commercial pilot logs many hours alongside a seasoned professional, so must a next-generation business leader take a patient, diligent approach to training and preparation. Proper mentoring and coaching is key to building confidence and competence in a next-generation business leader.

2 Pre-flight checks must be completed before take-off.

On any commercial flight a series of pre-flight checks are conducted to ensure the aircraft is fit to fly safely. Similarly, the most successful family businesses have a documented set of expectations for next-generation members in order to gauge their readiness for leadership positions. A pilot would never take off before the pre-flight inspection -- and you shouldn't assume that the next generation will be ready to take the controls without a training regimen.

3 Pilots take off into the wind.

While I don't profess to know a lot about physics or aerodynamics, I have noticed as I've flown that the pilot always looks to take off into the wind. As a human being who naturally seeks "the path of least resistance," I find this interesting. What I came to learn is that flying into the wind causes greater lift for the plane as it is taking off. This principle can also be seen in preparing the next generation for responsibility and stewardship of a family business or family wealth. Too many times, parents want their children to have an easier time than they did. They don't realize that it is actually more dangerous if the children are not strong enough to take off into the wind.

4 Runway length should correspond to the size of the airplane.

The amount of runway a plane needs to take off and land depends on the size and weight of the aircraft. Likewise, when a business is relatively small and lacks complexity, a transition might be successful without a lot of "runway." In larger, more complex organizations, the next-generation leader needs more seasoning to ensure success.

5 Consistent communication with air traffic control is mandatory.

Pilots wait for air traffic control to tell them when it is safe to approach the runway for takeoff or landing. The perspective of the person in the control tower is much broader; the controller knows the surrounding conditions and the potential dangers. It is the controller's job to coordinate the activity and to clearly communicate what is expected of the pilots so they can operate their aircraft safely.

In family companies, the senior generation commonly acts as the air traffic controller. They usually have a clear understanding of the business environment and are in the best position to make next generation leaders aware of the dangers. If the air traffic controller chooses not to communicate with the pilots, many people will be in danger and chaos will ensue around the airport. The same is true in a family business. Communication is key to ensuring a safe environment for future leaders. Follow these patterns for safe flying in your management transitions to the next generation and you will increase the likelihood that they will be confident and skilled enough to take the controls when the time is right.

A version of "Preparing for Takeoff" first appeared in Family Business Magazine in June 2011.

REFLECTIONS

_____

_____

_____

_____

_____

_____

_____

_____

_____

_____

_____

COMMITMENTS

_____

_____

_____

_____

Hemet Citrus Packing Plant

17

BECOMING VALUABLE

Attract what you expect. Reflect what you desire.
Become what you respect. Mirror what you admire.

—AUTHOR UNKNOWN

ave, are you an asset or are you a liability?" I was home from college during a break, talking with a friend about my walk-on status on the college basketball team. I immediately got defensive. "Of course I am valuable to the team," I reassured myself. "I work hard, and I show up everyday. That makes me valuable, right?" Maybe, but not necessarily. While hard work and consistent attendance are admirable traits, alone they are not enough to constitute value in the working world, and they won't be enough in family business either.

WHAT MAKES A PERSON VALUABLE?

Parents do not generally value their children because of performance, talent, or even behavior. A child is special because he or she is a part of the family. Ask employers about value, and they will equate it with skills, revenue, production and achievement. Such divergent definitions of "becoming valuable" are at the root of many family business issues. Value as a family member is inherent, but as a member of the business, it must be earned through education, experience and productivity.

Chances to confuse a person's "value" when working in a family business are plentiful. Children may have an unhealthy sense of entitlement or low self-esteem. In some cases the business may have poorly defined measures of "value" or worse, no measures at all for family employees. Family business owners struggle with the varying roles of disciplinarian, manager, equalizer, promoter and parent.

Understanding which of those roles to play can be tricky, but done thoughtfully it can also lead to enhanced communication, family harmony, independent children and incredible business opportunities.

COMMUNICATING ROLE DISTINCTION

Parents and children working together in the family business should explore and discuss the various roles they play (father/mother, husband/wife, hiring partner, CEO, etc). Misunderstandings occur in families when role distinction is blurred, so investing time in defining roles increases empathy and perspective on motivation behind actions.

Example: A child/employee asks his or her father/employer for the day off to go with friends to the lake. Dad/boss says no. Child/employee is upset. As a father, Dad may want his son or daughter to go and have fun, but as a business owner he knows there is essential work to be done. Is this case, should dad say "yes" or should he take care of the businesses' need to take care of the customer's order?

NEXT GENERATION ROLES AND OPPORTUNITIES WITHIN THE FAMILY BUSINESS

The next generation should approach their jobs as if their bosses aren't dad or mom. Expectations for enhanced pay, days off, etc. should not creep into the business. Children coming back to the business after graduation or working outside the business must be valuable to the company. Value as a child is not to be confused or equated with value as an employee or visa versa. Children should be welcomed into a family business because of the talent and value they can bring to the company, not because of their last name.

BECOMING VALUABLE

Valuable next generation additions are essential to long-term business success. A correct understanding of professional and personal roles will go a long way in maintaining healthy relationships within the business and the family.

Actively seeking skills, training and opportunities to use talents to further the mission of the company will add real value to the family-owned business and communicate that understanding.

The need to become valuable is just that: a need. And not just in business terms. The cost of not bringing value to the family business can include weakened family relationships or a business that loses its competitive edge. Perhaps more important is the confidence and resilience that a child stepping into a leadership position brings when she knows she is qualified, capable, and win or lose at the end of the day her daddy will always love her.

When thinking about the family business, remember this question: "Are you an asset or a liability?" Then focus your energy into those channels that will strengthen both your family and your business.

REFLECTIONS

_____

_____

_____

_____

_____

_____

_____

_____

_____

_____

_____

COMMITMENTS

_____

_____

_____

_____

SPECHT

18

CONCLUSION

The path towards generational continuity of your business will require work, but you can do it! It will require communication, but you can do that too! At times it will require individuals in your family to make sacrifices for the betterment of the group or the operation. The ultimate success of your process should be defined first by family relationships being preserved and second by a financially viable business being perpetuated.

There will be times of frustration and moments of uncertainty. The key to realizing your ultimate goal is to remember that this is a process, not an event. Your plans will need to evolve and change as your family and business grows. Surround yourself with advisers you trust and peers that can provide context to your succession planning experience.

Ultimately, family business continuity is a choice. No one can "make you" put a plan together. You can choose to do nothing or you can choose to do something. Many business owners choose to do noting for fear of creating conflict or to preserve harmony in the short-term. If that is what you choose, that is okay—if you are comfortable with the plan the government has laid out for your family business, doing nothing may be a fine alternative. But if you want to manage the expectations of your family members and control the ultimate ownership and management continuity of your operation, you must thoughtfully engage in this process.

The process should begin with determining the ideal outcome in your mind for the operation and for the family. After you have clarity with your future vision, engage professionals that will translate your desires into a technical plan. Share your thoughts with your family. Ask them for their feedback and then ask them to accept the plan that you create. Finally, review your plans regularly and update them as family and the operation evolves.

The world needs generational businesses to succeed. Your community needs your generational business to succeed. Your family's legacy depends on your choices. Be intentional about the success of your business. Get started today.

Dave + Taneil Specht - 2016

ABOUT THE AUTHORS

Dave and Taneil Specht are the parents of 5 children. Dave is a strategy consultant to generational family-owned businesses throughout the United States. He was a lecturer at The University of Nebraska and is best known for his creation of the Inspired Questions- For Family Business mobile app and the GenerationalBusiness360 process. Taneil is a university-educated woman that has chosen to invest her talents in the home. When she isn't chasing children, she is a writer, proofreader, sounding board and voice of reason in the entrepreneurial process.

To learn more about their work visit: *AdvisingGenerations.com*

THE STORY BEHIND THE PICTURE

1 **The Power of an Inspired Question**
This is a screenshot of the Inspired Questions- For Family Business App that is available on iOS and Android.

2 **A Case for Collaboration**
This is my son Damon after he came out of his 9-hour surgery where 2 surgeons, 3 hospitals and 10+ professionals collaborated to perform surgery at Doernenbecher Children's Hospital.

3 **Your New Lens**
This magnifying glass was found in Grandpa Wells' shop. This is something he and previous generations use when they are doing detail work on projects.

4 **Pioneers**
This is Makaley and Damon at the Historic Mormon Trail Center in Omaha, Nebraska learning about the pioneer story.

5 **Succession Planning Superheroes**
This is my four oldest kids showing off their superhero capes that Taneil made. These capes have been all over the United States and Europe teaching the superhero archetypes of business owners in transition.

6 **A Woman's Work-It's not what you think**
This is a Rosie the Riveter tin by J. Howard Miller. This tin is in our kitchen to show the strength and ability of women. Our family has some strong women!

7 **The Parable of the Ewer**
This is a large jug, otherwise known as a ewer. This was handcrafted by my good friend and master potter, Seth Green.

8 **Generational Business 360**
This is a picture of my grandpa Milton Curtis (far left) in front of Curtis & Sweet, his cabinet shop in Whittier, CA. Oddly enough he sold out to his business partner without asking his daughters about their interest in the business. Who knows, maybe I could have been a cabinetmaker.

9 **A Plane- Business Transition and the Private Plan Analogy**
This is a picture of one of the hangars at Duncan Aviation in the early days. Duncan Aviation, established in 1956 is the largest family-owned aviation maintenance company in the world. They are from Lincoln, NE and are great friends of the family. Photo provided by Todd and Connie Duncan.

10 Things to Consider Before Joining the Family Business
This picture is of one of the construction crews of Abel Construction. Hand mixing road material and still smiling. Abel Construction began in 1908 and is now known as Nebco Inc. in Lincoln, NE. Photo provided by Jim and Mary Abel.

10 **Unintended Consequences of Shared Ownership**
This is Jhett trying to pull his three older siblings in his wagon. He's working hard and they seem content to just be along for the ride. By the look on his face he doesn't seem convinced this is a good deal for him.

11 **Theft in the Family Business**
This is Damon taking some money from this vintage cash register. He's no thief, but he was recruited as the hand model for this photo shoot.

12 **The Quiet Killer of the Family Business**
This is me spending some time reading Grandma Melba a Dr. Seuss story. Grandma has dementia and the family takes turns caring for her. We love her so much!

13 **Sucker- Lessons in Communication**
This is Libby with a tight grip on her favorite suckers, Dum Dums™.

14 **The Compensation Conundrum**
This is a representation of many compensation packages in family businesses. There may be a car involved, some cash, a company credit card and almost always an "I Owe You."

15 **'I am not a sheep!'**
This is my son Reichert after his aunts dressed him up for our Nativity scene re-enactment at Grandma Wells' house. He thought he was being dressed up as a superhero, not a sheep. He wasn't happy!

16 **Preparing for Takeoff**
This is Bergen Eskildsen from Connell, WA in front of his families' airplane. The Eskildsen family has three generations of crop dusters. Photo provided by Bergen Eskildsen.

17 **Becoming Valuable**
This is a picture of the Hemet Citrus Packing Plant that was developed by one of my ancestors on my mom's side. His name was John Frazier.

SPECHT

APPENDIX

A version of "Pioneers" first appeared in Nebraska Bankers Magazine in November 2008.

A version of "Succession Planning Superheroes" first appeared in Family Business Magazine in November 2009.

A version of "A Woman's Work- It's not what you think" appeared in Successful Farming Magazine. March 2013. All Rights Reserved.

A version of "The Parable of the Ewer" first appeared in Campden Family Business in February 2012.

A version of "GenerationalBusiness360" first appeared in The Edge Magazine in May 2012.

A version of "A Plane- Business Transition and the Private Plan Analogy" first appeared in The Practitioner in October 2012.

A version of "Unintended Consequences of Shared Ownership" first appeared in Successful Farming Magazine in December 2013. Meredith Corporation. All rights reserved.

A version of "Theft in the Family Business" first appeared in Successful Farming Magazine in April 2013. Meredith Corporation. All rights reserved.

A version of "The Quiet Killer of the Family Business" first appeared in Successful Farming Magazine in September 2014. Meredith Corporation. All Rights Reserved.

A version of "Sucker- Lessons in Communication" first appeared in Nebraska Bankers Magazine in August 2010.

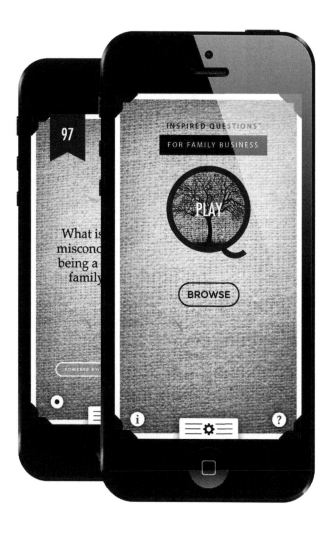

APPLICATIONS

PRESERVING THE WORLD'S MOST PRECIOUS ASSET: THE FAMILY BUSINESS. ONE CONVERSATION AT A TIME...

Generational Family Businesses represent the engine of the world economy. Planning for the continuity of these unique companies requires Inspired Questions, active listening and careful collaboration. Inspired Questions-For Family Business provides the platform that business-owning families will need to confront tough questions, explore perceptions, manage expectations as they implement a thoughtful strategy.

The App allows advisers to business-owning families to use E-mail, Messaging, Facebook and Twitter to facilitate these conversations with family members wherever they live.

Inspired Questions – For Family Business is being used by professional advisers (CPAs, Attorneys, Bankers, Insurance Professionals and Wealth Managers) and the business-owning families that they serve.